Sometimes Life Is Just Not Fair

Hope for Kids Through Grief and Loss

Reflections, prayers, and activities for children
(and for the child in each of us)
on loss and love, life and death,
and the presence of God always with us

Fr. Joe Kempf

Illustrated By Chris Sharp

Our Sunday Visitor Publishing Division
Our Sunday Visitor, Inc.
Huntington, IN 46750

Nihil Obstat
Msgr. Michael Heintz, Ph.D.
Censor Librorum

Imprimatur
✠ Kevin C. Rhoades
Bishop of Fort Wayne-South Bend
October 31, 2011

The *Nihil Obstat* and *Imprimatur* are official declarations that a book is free from doctrinal or moral error. It is not implied that those who have granted the *Nihil Obstat* and *Imprimatur* agree with the contents, opinions, or statements expressed.

The Scripture citations used in this book are from *The Holy Bible: Revised Standard Version.* Copyright © 1946, 1952, 1959, 1973 by the Division of Christian Education of the National Council of the Churches of Christ in the United States of America. All rights reserved. Used by permission.

Every reasonable effort has been made to determine copyright holders of excerpted materials and to secure permissions as needed. If any copyrighted materials have been inadvertently used in this work without proper credit being given in one form or another, please notify Our Sunday Visitor in writing so that future printings of this work may be corrected accordingly.

Our Sunday Visitor Publishing Division
Our Sunday Visitor, Inc.
200 Noll Plaza
Huntington, IN 46750
1-800-348-2440
bookpermissions@osv.com
PRINTED IN THE UNITED STATES OF AMERICA

ISBN: 978-1-61278-592-9
    (Inventory No. T1299)
LCCN: 2011945525

Cover design by Tyler Ottinger
Cover art: Chris Sharp
Interior design by Siok-Tin Sodbinow
Interior art: Chris Sharp

Graphics TwoFortyFour Inc., Wheaton, IL USA LT51174
January 2012

INSIDE THIS BOOK

Acknowledgments

This book has many authors, God.
Young, old, big, and small,
Each did their part with love and care.
Please, God, bless them all.

Everyone who helped with this
Has loved and then 'let go,'
They wanted to show others, God,
The hope that they now know.

Please bless them for the good
  they've done,
And help them know it's true
That through these pages
  they helped craft
Your people will find You.

If there is a child in your life… *(Introduction for parents, teachers and all entrusted with the care of children)*

> It's hard sometimes being orange
> It's hard sometimes being blue
> It's hard sometimes being me, oh God,
> You understand, don't You?

Sufferings come in many ways. We get confronted with our own diminishments and failure, or we bear the brunt of someone else's selfishness or cruelty. We meet the loneliness of not being included, or face the fear of a bad diagnosis. We see the pain we caused to people we love by what we've done or failed to do. Pets and people we love die. Dreams die also. Suffering visits us all; and, sometimes, the heartache is horrific.

This book addresses the tears in the heart of a child — whatever our ages. Though I am Catholic, grief is not. People of every race, language, religion, and way of life know heartache and loss.

Since it is such a universal suffering, this book looks especially at the grief that comes from death, and at the questions that surround it. You know them. If God is so good, why do innocent people suffer? What is our hope when facing the death of a loved one? What difference does it make to pray? What can we expect of ourselves — or others — when we are grieving? How do we talk to children about these things?

On the enclosed CD you can hear each of the ten prayers read by children, a few words with Fr. Joe, Big Al, Annie and friends, plus a song of farewell to a loved one.

While the essays in the back of the book are written specifically for parents, teachers, and all who love children, the reflections, activities, and prayers in the front of the book are for the children in our lives, and for the child in each of us.

5

Life is beautiful ... and so-o-o hard sometimes!

*L*ife is hard, isn't it? We might think that life should be easy, but it is not. Yes, there are many blessings in life. We each have so much to be grateful for! But for everyone, life is sometimes hard.

The tough times come in many ways. Maybe we get scary news about someone who is sick. Perhaps no one picked us for their team or invited us to play with them. Maybe our family is worried about money. A beloved pet dies. Sometimes WE get sick. Maybe Mom and Dad are fighting a lot, separating, or even divorcing. We see how other people suffer in our neighborhoods or around the world, and our hearts are sad for them. We feel lonely, think we are different, or get picked on. We have to move to a new school or home, or things change in other frightening ways. Sometimes we feel so many things inside, and we don't know what to do. For everyone life is hard.

But the good and bad things of life do not cancel each other out. At the very same time that life is hard, it is also beautiful! Just as our joys do not take away our sufferings, so our heartaches do not take away our blessings.

Some people go through life thinking only about the things that are painful. Others pretend like nothing hurts them. But everyone is blessed; everyone suffers. When we remember this, we might not be so shocked when we face tough times. And we will know that we are not the first, the last, or the only person for whom life is difficult.

Through it all, we need to remember that we are never alone. In good times and in bad, there is a Love that is always around us and always IN us. Our promise is that God understands … and will always be there to help us find a way.

"For everything there is a season."
Ecclesiastes 3:1

Sometimes Life Is Just Not Fair

It's hard sometimes being orange.
It's hard sometimes being blue.
It's hard sometimes being me, Oh God,
You understand, don't You?

Sometimes life is just not fair.
You know, God, what that's like,
When people hurt you through their words,
Or things don't turn out right.

Life has so much good in it,
Blessings big and small;
It also has some heartache
Woven through it all

So I pray to You, dear God,
Knowing that You care,
For when I bring my thoughts to You
I find You're always there.

No matter what this day might hold
Please show me what to do.
I really need You in my heart
So I can be like You.

- Each day holds some blessings and some hard things. What are two things that you are glad about today?

- What is one thing that you are NOT glad about today?

- Name one of your favorite feelings. Name one of your least favorite feelings.

- Many people can describe times when they sensed that God was with them. Can you describe a time when you could feel that God was with you?

Things to do

1. Draw a picture of the safest place you can imagine. Who would you put in that picture to be with you there? How does that place feel?

2. Some things can be both happy and sad at the same time. Ask people you trust to tell you about something they experienced that was both happy and sad.

3. Divide a piece of paper in half. On one side of the paper, write down some of the things that you think make God sad. On the other half of the paper, write down some of the things that you think make God happy. Hold that paper in your hand and say a prayer about what you wrote. You can say a prayer from memory (like the Our Father), make up a prayer in your own words, or use no words at all.

4. At the end of the day, look back and make a list of the ways you felt loved during the day.

Suffering is not God's idea

*W*hen life is hard, we might think it must be God's fault. It is not. God does not cause bad things to happen for any reason.

Yes, God is there in the bad times to help bring good out of them. But that does not mean that God caused someone to be sick, to suffer, or to die. Suffering is never God's idea, even though some of the things people say might make it sound that way. When we hear things like, "Everything happens for a reason," we need to remind ourselves that God did not make the hard thing happen. As a truly loving Father, God always wants what is best for us, but God never promised to protect us from all harm. The Holy Spirit is always calling us to be more loving and kind. But we are free, and God will never force us to live in a certain way. Our heartaches come from just being human, and from the ways we treat each other, but NOT from God.

The life of Jesus teaches us so much about our own lives.

Every December we celebrate Christmas. We remember that the Holy One — who created the world and all that is in it — became completely human as a little child. God knows what it is like to be us! Jesus laughed; he also cried. Jesus felt great joy; he also knew what it was like to be heartbroken. Jesus was the most loving person ever! But people betrayed him, made fun of him, and finally killed him. Every cross or crucifix we see reminds us that God understands a broken heart.

Whenever the painful times come, let us remember to turn to God honestly. We bring ourselves just as we are, and find that God is already there, understanding us, helping us, and holding us close.

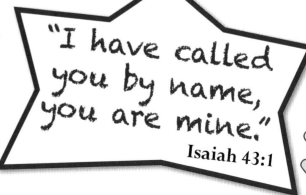

"I have called you by name, you are mine."
Isaiah 43:1

Your Name Is 'God'

Your name is 'God,' they say "You're great!"
That You are good and true.
But life has so much suffering.
Is that because of You?

Some think that all things are Your fault:
That You cause what is bad.
I know You'd never hurt us, God.
Our pain makes You so sad.

You always hear our heartfelt prayers,
You never go away.
You will help bring something good
From every painful day.

When life is hard or scary
We know that this is true.
You give us what we need, dear God;
You give the gift of YOU.

12

- How would you describe what God is like to someone who did not know God?

- If you could ask God one thing, what would you ask?

- Have you ever been angry at God? Why?

- How do you think you would have felt if you had been there and had seen Jesus on the cross?

Things to do

1. Draw a picture of one of the ways God might be there for someone having a hard time.

2. Jesus knows what it's like for us. He, too, laughed and cried, was angry, frightened, and excited. Think about something going on in your life, or in the life of someone you love, and share your feelings about these things in a letter to Jesus.

3. Say this prayer: "God, grant me the serenity to accept the things that can't be changed, the courage to change the things that can be changed, and the wisdom to know the difference."

4. Hold a crucifix in your hands and let it help you imagine how it must have felt to be there. Focus on Jesus. What would you say to him on the cross? As you see him there, say whatever you feel like saying to him.

God can bring good from ANYTHING

It might be one of the most amazing things of all, but God can bring good from anything! It might not be the cure we hoped for, or the exact thing we wanted. But, because God so loves us — and is ALWAYS with us — God can work a new good from any suffering we face.

We usually don't see it at once. But when bad things happen, we find help in surprising ways. Think of the loving people who were there to help us when we were sick, or to comfort us when we were sad. God is there for us through so many loving people.

And often, the new good that the Holy Spirit brings about is inside us. Sometimes it is in the difficult days that we let ourselves be more open to Love, and to becoming more like God. Many people will tell you that a suffering they experienced helped them understand more how to care for others who are sad

or hurting. And certainly WE are often part of the answer to someone else's prayer!

No, God does not prevent us from suffering, does not cure every illness, or does not stop people from doing mean things. But God is always with us. And God can bring good from anything.

"Be still, and know that I am God."

Psalm 46:10

So Many Things Are Different Now

Loving Father, hear my prayer.
I don't know what to do.
Many things are different now.
I really do need You.

So much is sad and scary.
I don't like this at all.
You ask me to be brave, dear God,
But what I feel is small.

I know You don't fix everything,
Or keep all harm away.
Instead, I know You help us, God:
You help us find a way.

When life is hard You hold us close.
You work through others, too.
Things might not be the way they were,
But You make something new.

- There are many sad things in the world. There is also much love. Describe a time when you felt that God was right there with you.

- Think about something bad that happened to you or your family (somebody got sick, you had to move, your house had a fire in it, etc.). Though we do not believe that God made those bad things happen, we do believe that God can bring good from them. Describe any good thing that came out of a bad or difficult situation.

- Finish this sentence: "If I were God…"

Things to do

1. Try to remember a time when you were sick. Draw a picture of some of the things that helped you feel better.

2. Hold a globe in your hands (or draw a picture of the earth), and, without using words, lift it up to God in prayer.

3. Find a magazine you can use and cut out pictures of where you "see" God every day. (For example: faces of a mom or dad, a doctor, a grandpa; nature; someone who is in need; etc.) Save these pictures and look again at them later. What else would you add now?

4. Write a letter to someone you know who is facing a difficult situation. What could you say to help them?

5. Draw a picture of you and God together. Tell others about your picture.

When someone dies

Everything that is living will die some day. Flowers and trees die. Our pets and the people we love die, too. Many things cause people to die. But people can't die because of anything we think or say. When someone dies, we often wish we could have done something to stop the person from dying, even when there was nothing we could have done or said that would have done so.

Dying is not like going to sleep, because when something alive goes to sleep, it can wake up again. In real life, unlike what we see on television or in video games, when someone dies, they can never come back. We might wish we could find a way to make them come alive again, but we can't.

If possible, when we know someone is dying, we can say truly important things like: "Thank you ... I'm sorry ... I forgive you ... Please pray for me ... I love you ... Goodbye."

Death is the end of living for a person's body. Their blood and muscles stop moving. The body of a dead person can't feel anything, eat or sleep, breathe or move. But there is another part of a person that can feel and think and love: the soul. This is what lives on!

A seed has to let go of being a seed before it can become a flower, and caterpillars let go of being caterpillars before they become butterflies. In the same way, when people die, they leave their bodies behind, so their spirits can go on living and be with God.

Saying goodbye to a person on earth is sad. But God taught us that there is a life beyond this life, and love is forever. Someday, in the world beyond this world, we can see our loved ones again.

"Fear not, for I am with you."
Isaiah 43:5

They Say His Life Is Ending, God

They say his life is ending, God;
His days on earth are done.
It's kind of sad and scary.
This "Goodbye" is no fun.

You say there's life beyond this life
Where he can be made new,
That when his life is over here
He gets to be with You.

Loving God, please take him home
And hold him in Your heart.
Make sure he knows we'll love him
Each day that we're apart.

Help us keep the best of him
Alive in what we do,
Until we meet him once again,
In our great home with You.

Things to think about or talk about

- If you could say anything you wanted to your loved one who has died, what would you say to them?

- What are three of the things that people often feel when someone they love dies?

- Who can you talk to when you are upset?

Things to do

1. Write words to remember a loved one who has died by completing these sentences:

   Today we gather to remember _____ _____.

   He/she is honored today for _____ _____.

   If we could, we would thank him/her for _____;

   We would tell him/her we were sorry for _____;

   We ask him/her to pray for us that _____.

   We will miss her/him, especially because _____.

2. Sometimes people feel guilty for things that are not their fault. No one can die because of something someone said or thought. If you know someone who blames themselves because someone they loved died, what could you say to help them?

3. Think of a loved one who is living, but who may be ill or very elderly. Write down what you would like to be sure to say to them while you still have the chance. What would you say you're sorry about? Grateful for? Willing to forgive? What do you love most about them? Send them your note, or, if possible, visit them, and tell them in person what you want to say.

21

There is a life beyond this life

*O*nce there were twins in their mother's womb. They were very happy there, and enjoyed the comfort of each other's presence. One day, things turned upside down for a moment. Afterward, when the one twin opened his eyes again, he saw that his brother was gone. He was so sad. Not only was this his twin, but also his best friend! And now, he was alone. How empty and lonely the womb seemed now.

But what he did not realize was that his brother had been born! He could not see the loving arms that were there to welcome his brother with joy at his birth. He did not really understand what it meant "to be born." All he knew was that his brother was gone, and his world seemed terribly empty and sad.

It is like that for us when someone we love dies. Our world seems so empty and cold. But, what we do not see is that our loved one has been born into the life beyond this life! We don't yet see the wonderful God who welcomes our loved one home.

It is indeed our faith that death is a birth into a new life. Heaven is not a physical place "up there," but is on the other side of everything we see. We don't know exactly what it will be like, but we can trust that it will be wonderful! "We will be with our awesome and loving God, and with all our brothers and sisters in Christ."

"I know that my redeemer lives."

Job 19:25

We do get tastes of heaven while we live on earth because God is always with us! In the loving goodness of people's hearts, in the wonders of life itself, in the miracles of forgiveness and love, we see a bit of the beauty of the life to come.

When someone we love dies, we pray for them, asking God to welcome them home, help their hearts grow to their fullness, and fill them with peace forever. Yes, there is a life beyond this life. At death, we are birthed into the arms of Love.

Love Does Not End

When our days on earth are done
It's sad to say, "Goodbye."
But there's a life beyond this life,
A home where we won't cry.

We bring what's best inside our hearts,
All that is good and true.
We leave our bodies on the earth
For we will be made new.

There is only goodness there,
Love and laughter, too.
And in Your home so beautiful
We get to be with You!

And everyone we care about
Is part of this great love,
There's so much joy and kindness there:
Below, around, above!

Although it's sad when someone dies
On this we can depend:
There is a life beyond this life
And love will never end!

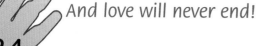

- What do you think heaven is like?

- Do you have any questions about your loved one's death, or about what will happen now? What are your questions, and whom would you like to ask?

- If you could tell everyone in the world something about your loved one, what would you say?

- Who believes in you?

Things to do

1. Create a blog where you share your memories of your loved one.

2. Find a song that gives you hope. After you listen to that song, say a prayer to God in your own words.

3. Write down a list of some things you see on earth that remind you of heaven.

4. Draw a picture of where you think your loved one who died is right now. Who else is there? What is it like?

5. Find something that reminds you of your loved one who has died. Show it to someone you trust and explain why it reminds you of him or her.

6. Imagine that your loved one who died was going to write a letter to you. What do you think they would say? Go ahead and write a letter to yourself from them.

What we do after a loved one dies

When a person dies, family members and friends will sometimes come by or call to offer support. Loving people understand that we are sad, and do what they can to show they care. Many families go to a funeral home that has rooms where they can be with one another. Friends come to remember the life of this person and to show their love.

When someone dies, we offer their soul to God, but we also take care of their lifeless body. The body looks similar to the person, but also very different, because the person's spirit is no longer in the body to make it look alive. We normally bury the body in the ground, or we sometimes cremate it, which means the body is turned into ashes. Burial and cremation are respectful ways to treat the body of the person who died. The person's body does not need to breathe, and it cannot feel anything, so these things do not hurt at all.

Most families also have a funeral service where they can pray for the one who died and for each other. We often feel so many emotions at this time, but underneath them all is our faith in a life beyond this life and that, because of God, our loved one lives on.

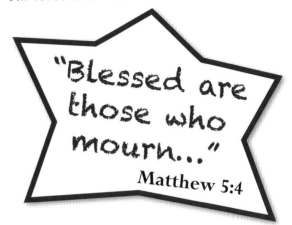

"Blessed are those who mourn..."
Matthew 5:4

At the service and at the funeral home, the body of the person who died is often there in a casket, or their ashes are in an urn. The cemetery is the place where we then take what remains of the body of our loved one to put in the earth. It is a place of holy memories, and sometimes people visit cemeteries to think about their loved one and to pray. And when we do so, it is good to remember that they are also praying for us!

Please, Dear God, We Need You

Things are weird in my life, God.
Not like they used to be.
I'm not sure how to live these days,
Or how to best be me.

Death has changed so much, dear God,
Our plans are different, too.
There is sadness in our hearts
In everything we do.

Grown-ups cry, and then they laugh,
I do the same thing, too.
I'm feeling lost and scared inside,
And so I pray to You.

I bring, dear God, what's in my heart
And all who hurt this day.
I know that I sure need Your help
With all my heart, I pray.

You promise to be with us, God.
You'll never go away.
So many things are changing now,
But You are here to stay.

- If you have ever been to a funeral, cemetery, or funeral home, describe what that was like for you.

- If you had the chance to plan the funeral for your loved one, what would you include? Is there a special song you would like? A favorite reading from the Bible? Something you would want to be said?

- What are two good ways to show that you are angry?

- How do you like people to help you when you are sad?

- What would you say to someone who is afraid to cry in front of other people?

Things to do

1. Draw a big heart. Then write inside the heart some of the things you liked about the person who died. Let it remind you that your special person who died is always in your heart.

2. What is something that your loved one liked to do? Is there anything that you liked to do with them? If you can, do one of those things even though that person is not there, and whisper a prayer for them while you do it.

3. What is a song that makes you think of your loved one who died? Why?

4. If you could send an email to God, what would you write? If you could attach a picture, what picture would you send to God? Why would you send that picture?

God understands a broken heart

When someone we love dies, the world is changed forever. There is an empty place in our hearts that no one else can fill.

At times like this, no one can know exactly what it is like for us. Even though our feelings can be painful, it is better to be aware of them than to act like we don't have them at all.

There are many things that people feel when someone dies. Some get angry and think that it is not fair. Many people regret some of the things they said or didn't say. We might get scared or feel lonely.

For some, one of the worst things is watching other family members be sad. If the person suffered for a long time, we might be relieved that they are no longer in pain, even though we are sad that they died. We often feel opposite things at the same time!

Sometimes you might think you caused someone to die because of things you felt or said. It is not your fault, even if you ever thought about them dying, because words and thoughts cannot cause a person to die. It is okay to be afraid sometimes, but it is good to remind yourself that you will be okay. You will have all that you need.

Usually it is good to share our feelings with people we trust and to let them help us. Sometimes people say things to us like, "Be strong" or "Don't cry," but crying is a strong and brave thing to do. Our tears are a sign of something good. We wouldn't cry if we didn't care! Jesus cried when his friend died. God understands a broken heart. It is also okay to laugh. You don't have to think about what happened or feel sad all the time.

When we are sad because we miss a loved one who has died, we can always ask God to give them a hug for us. The good news is that love is forever. And God is always there!

"Jesus wept."
John 11:35

31

My Heart Is Sad; I Miss Her So

My heart is sad; I miss her so.
The world is not the same.
I miss the way she looked and smelled,
The way she said my name.

Dear God, the world seems darker now.
There's so much in my heart,
I wonder how I'll be okay
Since we are now apart.

No one else could take her place.
She means so much, you see.
Please tell her that I love her, God.
Give her a hug for me.

Things to think about or talk about

- Jesus cried when his friend died. How does it feel to know that?

- Sometimes sadness feels like hurt in our bodies. Where in your body does it hurt now?

- When someone we love dies, we feel so many things. What is it like to be you, right now?

- While no one can completely understand all that you feel, there are people who care and understand. Who can you talk to who cares about how you are?

Things to do

1. Make a memory book or website to honor your loved one who died.

2. Invite your family to include your loved ones who died by name in your meal prayer.

3. Write a letter to your loved one who died. Include sentences that begin:

   ___ Some of the things I miss about you are …

   ___ I'm sorry for…

   ___ I'm angry about…

   ___ I forgive you for…

   ___ I thank you for …

   ___ Please pray for me that…

4. Each cartoon below describes a feeling. Find the pictures that show the way you feel today. What else do you feel? Tell someone you love about your feelings.

Going on with hope

"*I* just want it to be the way it was." Many people feel this way when a loved one dies. So many things are different, and we feel such a mixture of painful emotions. Yet it seems that other people's lives go on as if nothing happened.

Many people might not realize all the things we feel inside. They might not know what to say, or may be afraid to talk about our loved one who died. We might have to tell them whether or not we would like to talk about it.

Sometimes we feel upset or cry when we do not expect to. Or we may be surprised when we do not think about it for awhile. This is normal. This is okay.

When someone we love dies, our world is changed forever. But our world has not ended. Though we can't go back to the way it was before, we can find a new way to live and love in this world. We have the two things we need most: 1) We are loved, and 2) We can love. No matter what happens in life, these two things will help us go on.

In honor of a loved one who died, some find it helpful to write a letter to the person who died, to draw a picture for them, or to think of them as they sing or dance. Many do something that the loved one used to do, or reach out in kindness in honor of them. Part of our job is to keep the best of them alive in our hearts by how WE live!

The hard part about dying is that the person is not coming back. The good part is that we are still connected and can pray for each other. They love us: we love them.

Sadness isn't forever. Love is!

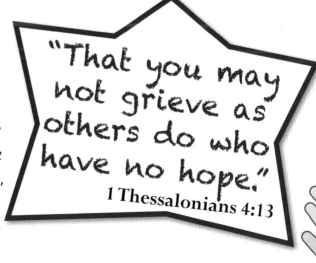

"That you may not grieve as others do who have no hope."
1 Thessalonians 4:13

My World Will Never Be the Same

My world will never be the same
Now that she's gone from me.
Dear God, I truly need You,
Please show me how to be.

She would want me to go on,
And live my life each day.
She would tell me it's okay
To laugh and love and play.

Please help me keep the best of her
Alive inside my heart.
That in the days I'm given here
I'll also do my part

To make this world a better place
Just like she did, You see.
Take good care of her, dear God,
And hear her prayers for me.

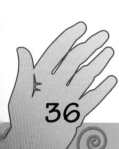

- If you could create a web page for your loved one who died, what would you put on it?

- How are you a better person because of your loved one who died?

- God put goodness in everyone, but no one is perfect. What is something that your loved one did that you think was a mistake? What is something about them that you did not like?

- What is one thing for which you would say "Thank you" to your loved one?

Things to do

1. Make a list of five things you can do that usually make you feel better.

2. You can still celebrate your special person's birthday even though he/she died. Honor your special person's birthday with a card or a birthday wish.

3. Pick a song that seems to understand some of what you feel inside. With whom would you like to share that song?

4. If you could write a prescription to help a person with a broken heart, what would you recommend they should do to take care of themselves?

5. Ask your family or friends to set aside a special time to remember your loved one who died. You can share memories, and perhaps do one of those things that the person loved to do.

6. Have someone with a video camera interview you and make a news report to tell the world what your loved one was like. End with a message to everyone who is sad.

37

How to help someone who is sad

When something bad happens, it often seems like the whole world has become dark. During those times, just a little bit of light can make such a difference. Jesus counts on US to bring the light of his love to them. Some people aren't sure what to do or say when someone is hurting. But, if someone is sad, it is so important that we reach out to them. We might bring just the little bit of light they need to be okay.

One of the best things that we can do for others is simply to be there. We don't try to fix them, or take away their sadness. We just let them know we care.

We have to be careful about what we say. It usually does not help people if we say such things as, "Don't cry," or "I'm sure that God did this for a good reason," or "I know exactly how you feel."

Sometimes it's best just to tell them we're sorry, hold their hand or give them a hug. Maybe we simply sit with them, or play with them. This way we let them know they are not alone. If the person cries — or if we do — remember that crying is not bad. It is a sign that we care.

If we do not personally know the one who died, it is often good to ask the person to tell us about their loved one and what he or she was like. Also, it is good to remember that times like holidays and birthdays can be extra sad for those who have had loved ones die.

When we reach out to those who are hurting we work together with God to make their world a little brighter. The love in our hearts for them is not just what God is like; it actually is God loving them through us!

"Love one another as I have loved you."

John 15:12

My Friend Is Feeling Sad These Days

I really need Your help, dear God,
To do what must be done.
My friend is feeling sad, these days.
She seems to need someone.

Sometimes words don't help at all.
I wonder what to do.
I want to be a friend to her
And love her like You do.

Maybe I'll just sit with her
And let her know I care.
I pray that through my time with her
She'll know that YOU are there.

- Write a letter to someone that you know who is sad or hurting. What could you say to help them?

- Was there ever a time when you were sad and someone helped you? What did they do?

- There are many ways to bring Jesus' love to the world. How can you bring love…

  a. with your hands?

  b. with your heart?

  c. with your eyes?

  d. with your ears?

  f. with your words?

Things to do

1. Think of those you know who have had a loved one die or who experienced another loss. Put their names and special dates on a calendar to remind yourself to call or write to them.

2. Write a list of some people who need extra prayers. Put that list in a special place and, from time to time, look at that list to remind you to pray for those people.

3. Think of someone in your school or neighborhood who sometimes gets picked on, ignored, or made fun of, and go out of your way to say something kind to them that you wouldn't normally say.

4. Fill in the conversation bubbles.

Speaking Love

Prayer and the presence of God

*T*here is nothing we could ever experience, no place we could ever go, where God is not already there. God is always and everywhere present to us, but we are not always present to God!

Prayer is all about becoming present to God. This means that – when we pray - we need to bring an openness in our hearts to more than just our own thoughts and feelings. In prayer we become aware of the Holy One, of God. This time with God helps us become more LIKE God!

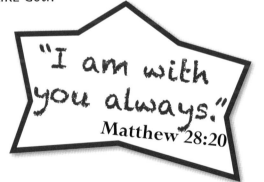

"I am with you always."
Matthew 28:20

There are many ways to pray. Sometimes we pray with other people in Church. Or we can pray all by ourselves. We can pray prayers from memory such as the Lord's Prayer, or we can talk with God in our own words, just like with a friend. Our prayer does not need to be fancy or pretty. It needs to be honest and humble. And sometimes we pray without words at all, just sitting quietly in God's presence.

We can pray anywhere: outdoors, indoors, standing, kneeling, sitting, even on a bicycle! Sometimes we might pray out loud, or other times just in our heads and hearts. We don't usually hear God speak back to us with words. But we can learn to sense how God does come to us: sometimes in silence, perhaps in a gentle nudge in our hearts, maybe in a new way of thinking, or just simply in knowing that we are in the loving presence of Someone other than ourselves.

No, prayer does not mean that the world around us will always change in the ways we are wishing. But we can be sure that God is with us, and hears us when we pray. For the best "result" of prayer is this: when we seek God, we will find God!

In Good Times and in Bad

Life has so much heartache, God,
And countless blessings, too.
In good times and in bad times
You show us what to do.

We help each other on the way.
We care for those left out.
We do our best to love this world.
That's what it's all about.

And each step of the journey, Lord,
No matter where we go,
You surround us with Your love.
You're always there, we know,

So help us God to live our days
With hearts and actions true.
In good times and in bad times, God,
Please help us be like You.

Things to think about or talk about

- Pretend that AWESOMEGOD@ UNIVERSE.WOW was God's email address. What other email addresses could you create for God?

- WHY do we pray?

- What is the best time of the day for you to have quiet time with Jesus? Where would you go to have this quiet time with him?

- How do you pray? What helps you?

- Have you ever been looking for God but felt like God wasn't there? Where do you think God was?

Things to do

1. Take clay (or some other material) and form an image that shows something of God's relationship with you. Keep this image and repeat this activity several months from now. How do your two images compare?

2. Make a prayer table, such as a special little table or corner of your dresser, where you put things that often remind you of God.

3. Go to a beautiful place. Close your eyes, then — with eyes closed — open each of your senses one at a time: first smell; then taste; then touch; then hearing; and only then, while aware of each of the other senses, also open your eyes. With or without words, whisper a prayer.

46

For parents, teachers, and all who love children

Life is beautiful ... and so-o-o hard sometimes

- Grieving children sometimes think they are now "different" or that they don't fit in. We can help assure them that they are not alone.

- One of the greatest spiritual truths we can teach our children is that this world is "both/and," not "either/or." Our children need to know that the blessings and heartaches of life don't cancel each other out.

- Grief denied comes at a great price. If we don't deal with grief, it will deal with us, and the consequences can be serious.

- As followers of Christ, we do well to keep grateful hearts, for we are blessed indeed. Our sufferings do not erase the fact that — in the big scheme of things — THERE IS ALWAYS MORE REASON FOR JOY THAN NOT.

- At baptism, we are marked with the Sign of the Cross. This is to remind us, in part, that we will suffer, but that we will never suffer or die alone. We are baptized into Christ's death and resurrection, and are now part of his family.

- The shortest sentence in the Bible is this: "Jesus wept." It is also one of the most poignant.

- St. Ephraim once said, "Until you have cried, you do not know God." There is something in the heart of God that we will only understand when we ourselves can weep. For when we care enough that we would hurt for love, that love in our heart is not only what God's love is like but actually IS God's love.

Suffering is not God's idea

- God does not cause suffering for any reason.

48

- Much of the suffering of the world is the direct result of sinful human choices, individually or collectively: selfishness; lack of forgiveness; or the violence we inflict upon one another. We humans are, by far, the greatest cause of suffering in the world.

- Sin by its very nature hurts us, and others. When we choose sin, we choose the harm that is the consequence of that sin. God is not somewhere "out there" waiting to inflict suffering as punishment for our sin.

- God does NOT cause suffering to bring good out of it. Clichés such as "God never gives you more than you can handle" and "Everything happens for a reason" can give us a distorted image of God. Many will never truly know the wonder of God because they've been told God sent them a tragedy for some "better reason."

- The only way God could keep us all from suffering is to remove our free will. But God is radically committed to our free will and will not force us to be loving or just.

- There is no satisfactory or rational answer to the question "Why?" in the face of the sufferings caused by disease and accidents. God is wonderfully alive in the world for us at every moment. Yet our very human nature is frail and full of suffering. Illness, injury, death, and accidents are all a part of our limited, frail human condition. They are not something God wills upon us for any of the reasons so commonly suggested.

- God created us with the ability to love. In this, God gave us the capacity for the other suffering, the great suffering that is at the center of God's own heart: the freely chosen suffering of love.

God can bring good from ANYTHING

- "I am with you always." In these words from the end of Matthew's Gospel we hear the promise of Jesus that there is no place we can go, no situation we could ever find ourselves in, in which God is not already there filled with love for us, holding us close.

- Though God does not cause us to suffer, as our Scriptures teach us, God

does "make all things work to good," even our pain and loss! Because God has embraced our sufferings, God can give them meaning and bring from

them a much greater good than we can imagine.

- In the midst of our suffering, it is always a leap of faith to choose to trust that God can bring good from this pain. Jesus himself cried from the cross: "My God, my God, why hast thou forsaken me?" (Mark 15:34).

- Our crosses are more than obstacles. Within our very sufferings is the promise of transformation, of resurrection! Indeed, it is often brokenness itself that opens our hearts so that we can truly meet God.

- In light of the death and resurrection of Jesus, the questions "Why?" and "Why did this happen to me?" need ultimately to give way to the bigger question: "Now what?" Given this reality of pain or suffering, now how will I live? In the midst of tragedy and loss can I choose to trust the God who is always working a greater good beyond anything I can see? Now what? Now where is love? Now what am I called to do or to be? Now how do I go on?

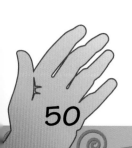

When someone dies

When someone is dying…

- Sometimes a loved one dies suddenly and without warning. Other times, we have advanced knowledge that someone we love is facing death. This awareness, while heart-rending, also provides great opportunity, and we need to be intentional about how we will live the remaining time.

- If possible, it is a great gift for us — AND OUR CHILDREN — to say these important things to the dying person: "I forgive you; I'm sorry; thank you; I love you; goodbye."

- The greatest gift we have to offer someone who faces death is our loving presence. They do not need religious clichés. They do not need someone to "cheer them up." They need us — as we are — with a willingness to be with them as they are.

- In the final stages of a person's dying, it is good to presume that they can still hear us. It is important

to continue to love them with our touch, our silence, our tears, and our words of love, prayer, and encouragement. We trust that, on some level, the person who is dying is aware of our love.

- Sometimes, it is important to tell a loved one who is dying that it is "okay to let go." Those words of permission, along with our love, forgiveness, and prayer can help the dying person move from the love in this life to the love that awaits them in the next.

After someone dies … telling a child about death

- If possible, it is good for a child to be told of death by a parent, or someone the child knows and trusts. It is good to tell them as soon as possible after the death.

- Be sure to give simple, honest, brief, and straightforward answers. It is important to use the words "dead" and "died." It is okay to say, "I don't know."

- To describe death, it might be good to say things like: "When a person dies, their spirit leaves their body, and his or her body stops working. They no longer breathe or move or eat, and that is forever."

- Do not burden the child by suggesting that they need to be strong now, that they should "be the man or woman of the house," or that they should not cry.

- Children are often very literal. Telling children that the one who died "fell

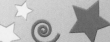

asleep" often creates anxiety about sleeping. We tell children — and rightly so — that our loved ones are still with us in spirit. Yet if we say that "Daddy is always watching over you," some children will worry that daddy physically sees everything they do. Nor is it good to say, "God needed another angel," or "God only takes the good ones," because such phrases mislead them about God.

- It is also important to address these often unspoken questions: "Did I make that person die?" "Will you die now?" "Will I die now?" "Who will take care of me now?"

There is a life beyond this life

- As the Catholic funeral liturgy says: "Life is changed, not ended. When the body of our earthly dwelling lies in death we gain an everlasting dwelling place in heaven."

- Heaven is not a physical place "up there," but rather a state of complete union with God and our brothers and sisters in Christ. St. Paul tells us that the life beyond this life will

be even more wonderful than we can imagine: "What no eye has seen, nor ear heard, nor the heart of man conceived, what God has prepared for those who love him" (1 Corinthians 2:9).

- Our creedal belief in "the resurrection of the body" sustains our hope for our unity with our loved ones beyond this life. Perhaps the scriptural accounts of Christ's body after his resurrection give us a way to start to understand what our own resurrected bodies will be like.

- This chapter's image of the twins in their mother's womb can be a help to introducing the concept of life after death. The term "womb" might be new for some children, and, of course, it is always important — when possible — to check in on children's understanding of the various concepts and terms they encounter.

- Death does not end a relationship. The great Easter promise of life beyond death helps us know that — even now — we are connected with our loved ones who have died.

- We pray for our loved ones who have died, not to convince God to love them, for God already does that more than we can imagine. But rather, our love and prayers are an aid to their completion, to empower them more fully to open up to receive the embrace of God's great healing love.

- Our loved ones who have gone before us grow more alive in God, and are in a very real way "cheering us on," pulling for us, praying for us. It is good to pray for our loved ones who have died ... and to receive from them their love and prayers.

What we do after a loved one dies

- In most cases it is wise to bring children to the hospital, the funeral home, the funeral service, and the cemetery. All of these can help bring closure and needed perspective for the children. In addition, children have vivid imaginations and can often create images of all of this that are much more frightening than the reality.

- We help our children greatly if we let them know what to expect, answer their questions, and check in with them throughout these events.

- Drawing a picture for, or writing a note to, the person who died can be very helpful for children. Using clay, paint, or other materials can help children express feelings and thoughts without words. Since we will often not understand what they have created, asking them to tell us about

it provides still another opportunity for expression and communication.

- Younger children have short attention spans and can go from weeping to playing in a very short time. Because this is normal and healthy, during service and visitation times, it is wise to find an adult or two to be with the child; request a room for the children to play in; and perhaps provide materials for writing or creating something in memory of their loved one.

- Children often find it helpful if they are allowed to pick out some belongings of the deceased to keep for their very own. A memory box with such items can help by providing a tangible connection to the deceased and a focal point for their memories.

- One of our jobs is to help children know the good news: that love is forever … and God is always with us.

God understands a broken heart

- When someone we love dies, our lives are changed forever. There is a pain and loneliness at the death of a loved one that is often unimaginable — except to

those who have themselves lost deeply. It has been accurately said that no one ever really can understand.

- It is common to feel contradictory emotions simultaneously. Also, we often have feelings about our feelings.

- We do not need to always "be strong," or "keep ourselves together," in the presence of children. When we are honest about our own feelings around them we allow children to grieve as well. However, children are not meant to be our caregivers. And if children see intense grief in their parents, they might need to be reassured that Mom or Dad will still be able to take care of them.

- How we grieve will vary according to how different we each are; what our relationship was like with the person who died; and how they died. There is no correct way to grieve, and no time limit.

- To talk about "stages of grief" might be misleading to some, because it seems to suggest that there is an ordered progression that needs to be followed. It is perhaps better to say that there are a number of elements and dimensions to the experience and process of grief.

- In a classroom setting, it is important to acknowledge the death of a student's loved one. However, the student should not forever be "the one whose loved one died." It can be of great help to the other students

in the class if there is time when the bereaved child is not there, to ask them if it is okay that the bereaved student cries, and whether it is also okay if sometimes he or she laughs.

- Grief can be especially complicated when someone died because of suicide. Grief in this situation is often accompanied — more than typically so — by anger at the person who took their own life, and guilt that we did not do something to prevent their death. Also, there is often less support for those whose loved ones die this way than for those whose loved ones die from some other cause.

- It is common that children will blame themselves for the death of someone they knew. It is good to bring this up, even if they don't.

- Children often express anger about the death. They may feel angry with God. They may blame a family member because they are near and are "safe" targets. They may even feel angry with the person who died for leaving them.

- Children process things differently according to their age and temperament. Though children are usually resilient, they will likely revisit their grief anew in different ways, according to their age or stage of development.

Going on with hope

- When someone we love dies, or when we suffer any major loss, we do not "get over it." Our lives are changed forever.

We figure out how to continue. We learn new ways to be okay. But we will not be the same.

- Grief has been well described as coming like "waves": It pounds us for a while; then it is calm. It pounds us again; then it is calm. Over the years, the waves typically come a little less frequently and a little less intensely, but they still come. Often we cannot predict what will trigger them.

- If some of the images from the time of death were frightening or painful, those images will usually lessen somewhat over time, and more frequently be replaced by images and memories that are more pleasant.

- Many people dread holidays, anniversaries, and other special events that involved their loved one. It is good to decide in advance on rituals that you will use to help remind you of your loved one — for example, a special candle at meal prayers, a memory table, a birthday cake, etc.

- Often a trusted counselor is crucial. For example, the death of a child is often extremely difficult on married couples. Finding a trustworthy counselor to walk a couple through grief and to help them understand its effect on marriage can sometimes be essential.

- As much as possible, it is important to choose those things that we know usually help us during difficult times. Keeping a healthy balance of nutrition, sleep, and exercise is important. Addictive or destructive behaviors will only make things worse. The support of people we trust can be invaluable. Perhaps, as with prayer, the best we can do is to simply be available for the healing that comes through grace over time.

- In response to the death of a loved one, and all that it stirs up inside us, we need to remember that it is okay to laugh and be happy! It is also okay to weep. And it is certainly okay to miss a loved one for the rest of our lives.

How to help someone who is sad

- It is our calling to help those who suffer know that God is with them. We do that best by our presence, by our willingness to be with others in their suffering. Being present to someone in their struggles does not mean we to try to fix them or the situation. It means, rather, that we listen to their pain, and walk with them during the difficult times. Presence is the most important gift we can give.

- We need to think ahead about what we really want to say to those who have had a loss. It is not a good idea to say things such as: "Don't cry," or "I'm sure that God did this for a good reason," or "I know exactly how you feel."

- Usually, the best thing to say is simply, "I'm sorry," and then be quiet and maybe hold the person's hand, and listen.

- If we do not personally know the person who died, it is often good to ask the grieving to tell us about their loved one and what he or she was like.

- Holidays, birthdays, and anniversaries can be intensely painful for those who have lost loved ones, and often for years to come. We do well to contact those who are grieving and tell them we are aware that they are spending this occasion without their loved one, and to let them know we are wondering how they are doing.

- When we call or offer help, we often say, "Please let me know if there is anything I can do." That approach, though well intentioned, is usually not effective. Instead, it is much better if we first listen to our own hearts, decide what we want to offer, and then make that offer specifically.

- When we face the suffering of the world, we stand before great mystery. But we do not stand alone, without hope, or without something to offer. By how we love one another we help make real the promise that, no matter what we suffer, God will be there.

Prayer and the presence of God

- Always and everywhere, God is present to us. However, we are not always present to God. In prayer, we develop a way of seeing and hearing that opens us to more than the chattering of our own thoughts and feelings. In prayer, we make ourselves available to meet The Other, the Holy One, God.

- Clearly Jesus was a person of prayer, and on more than one occasion Jesus taught us to pray. But what do we expect to happen when we pray? The best and truest "result" of authentic prayer is this: When we seek God, we will find God! That encounter will ultimately change us.

- Certainly, when someone we love is ill or suffering, it is good to bring that person to God in prayer. With or without words we hold our loved ones and all our cares before God, trusting that God, like a truly loving

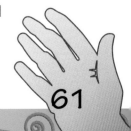

61

parent, hears us and is moved. By focusing the energy of our intentional awareness, perhaps we become more open vessels of God's grace for the world. Certainly, as we grow as members of the body of Christ, the entire body of Christ is blessed.

- Miracles clearly were not the primary focus of Jesus' ministry. The healings and cures that Jesus accomplished were signs of the in-breaking of the reign of God, and the ultimate victory of love over hatred, life over death. Jesus wanted his miracles to lead people more deeply into God and God's way, but in response people often only looked for more miracles.

- Miraculous cures do not seem to be the primary work of God now any more than they were at the time of Jesus. Though God only wants life for us, the reality of our human condition is that all people suffer, all people die. Our faith does not call us to believe that people will be healed of their suffering. But rather that — when someone is suffering — all the love in the universe is present to them! What they most deeply need is already theirs. Sometimes the miracle is in realizing that this is true.

- In our prayer it is important to be open to the good beyond what we specifically prayed for. Sometimes, when we are looking for a cure, we might not see the greater healing that God offers. The greatest miracles Jesus worked — and continues to work — are the changing of people's hearts.

Beyond what you can see

A song of "goodbye" to a loved one …

There is a new home for you
Beyond what you can see
You don't have to be afraid
You've felt its love in me

This loving place of goodness
Is filled with such pure light
You will truly be at peace
And Love will hold you tight

Go to God, my precious love
Know I'll always care
One day we will hug again
When I join you there

When I wonder how I'll live
Without you being here
I'll know that you will pray for me
And trust that you are near

You will always have my heart
You know I love you, too
Yes, we're both forgiven
And now we start anew

Go to God, my precious love
Know I'll always care
One day we will hug again
When I join you there

"Sometimes Life Is Just Not Fair" - Audio CD

- A few words with Fr. Joe, Big Al, Annie and friends - Track 1
- Prayer One: Life is beautiful … and so-o-o hard sometimes – Track 2
- Prayer Two: Suffering is not God's idea – Track 3
- Prayer Three: God can bring good from ANYTHING – Track 4
- Prayer Four: When someone dies – Track 5
- Prayer Five: There is a life beyond this life – Track 6
- Prayer Six: What we do after a loved one dies – Track 7
- Prayer Seven: God understands a broken heart – Track 8
- Prayer Eight: Going on with hope – Track 9
- Prayer Nine: How to help someone who is sad – Track 10
- Prayer Ten: Prayer and the presence of God – Track 11
- The song: "Beyond What You Can See" – Track 12

Child readers:

- Katherine Kempf
- Andrew Tabora
- Ashna Mahadev
- Yael Aguayo
- Mikayla Kempf

"Beyond What You Can See" – Written by Fr. Joe Kempf

- Cathy Pescarino, vocals
- Keith Wehmeier, vocals
- Larry Groeblinghoff, vocal harmony
- Shawn Williams, violin
- Christina Hunt, oboe
- Kelsey Rhoades, flute
- Matthew Geary, recording engineer
- Mark Sacco, piano and keyboards
- Children's audio – Custom Video Productions